AF439563

C'MA AND PAPA'S HOUSE:

AN ABC BOOK FOR BRAVE KIDS

WRITTEN BY:

DR. CELESTINE MCNEAL

ILLUSTRATED BY: BILAL TAHIR

Cover design by Bilal Tahir

Interior design by Bilal tahir

Editing by Lattifa Bryant

Published by Lattifa Bryant, Build Your Own Books Publishing

Printed in United States

First Edition: 2023

This book is dedicated to my beloved grandchildren whose love, wisdom, and
guidance continue to inspire me every day.
Thank you for helping Cma and Papa create a home filled with warmth,
 laughter, and cherished memories.

For more information, please visit:

www.drcelestinemcneal.com

For inquiries on building your book, visit www.buildyourownbooks.com
Email: info@buildyourownbooks.com

Are you ready for a journey that is oh so bold, inside of C'Ma and PaPa's house made of gold? Bluelle and Nasir will be your guide, as we go on a journey with surprises waiting inside. In each room, an adventure unfolds, using the alphabet for our stories untold. Through every challenge, we will stand tall, with bravery and strength, we will conquer all. Thank you C'Ma and PaPa, our guiding light, for inspiring us to reach new heights. In C'Ma and PaPa's house, a world of wonder and play, with love and courage, we will soar each day. Turn the page and let the adventure begin in this exciting story that will make you grin.

A is for the Apples, juicy and sweet,
a delicious treat that we love to eat.
With a crunch and a munch, we take a bite,
savoring the flavor with all our might.

B is for Bananas, the yellowest treat.
This is one fruit that can't be beat.
Anytime of the day, they bring us joy,
especially before going out to play, oh boy!
We peel it open, take a bite so sweet,
Bananas are the perfect energy boost we need.
E.B.B KIDS
E.B.B KIDS
2

C is for the Couch where we love to play,
jumping up and down, having fun all day.
With cushions to bounce on and pillows to hug,
we giggle and laugh, feeling cozy and snug.
E.B.B KIDS
E.B.B KIDS

"Don't jump on the couch!" with a big loud D!
C'ma and Papa say, reminding us– you see.
They want us to be safe and keep things neat,
so we find other games to play on our feet.

E is for Elephant, big and strong, standing in
CMa's living room where it belongs. With a trunk
so long and ears so wide, it fills
our house with joy and pride.

F is for the Frogs, croaking by the pool
as their sounds fill the night and it's really cool.

G is for Good because we always try our best,
even when the summer heat puts us to the test.

7

H is for the Heat that comes from the sun,
and we soak it up and play until the day is done

Our next stop is the fridge where we sneak for some ICE,
Hiding from C'ma and Papa, our secret delight!

J is for Jack in the box, what a surprise!
We saw it on TV, with joy in our eyes.
It pops up and wiggles, oh what a sight!
Bringing laughter and giggles, filling
the room with light.

K is for Keys we played with as babies,
a jingly-jangly bunch, driving us crazy!
We'd grab them and shake, making our own songs,
hiding keys from C'ma and Papa– we were so wrong.

L is for Love that we say every day,
It's a special feeling that never
goes away. With hugs and
smiles, and words so true,
Love is what we share with you.
E.B.B KIDS
E.B.B KIDS

M is for our Moms, the best mothers around,
With hearts so warm, their love knows no bound.
They are always there, with a comforting embrace,
guiding us through life's every chase.
E.B.B
E.B.B
KIDS
E.B.B
KIDS

N is for "No," when Cma and Papa say so.
They guide us and help us learn and grow.
With wisdom and love, they set the way,
teaching us right from wrong day to day.

O is for Oven, hot and bright and we stay away from it,
day and night.
Its flames and heat can cause a burn, so we are
cautious and we always learn. We let C'ma and
Papa handle it with care, keeping
our hands and fingers aware.

15

P is for Popcorn, a tasty treat,
With CMa and PaPa, it's always sweet.
The kernels pop, bursting with flavor,
enjoying this snack, we LOVE the flavor.
With CMa and PaPa, it's always a pleasure
to munch on popcorn, a timeless treasure.

Q is for Queen, our C'ma so dear.
Queen is a title she holds with love and cheer.
With grace and beauty, she leads the way,
guiding us through each and every day.

R is for Rockets, ready to fly
up in the sky, so very high.
With fire and fuel, they
zoom through space,
exploring new planets at
an incredible pace.

S is for Sun, shining in the sky, waking us up as it rises up high. With its bright rays, it brings us light, chasing away the darkness, oh so bright!

T is for Time-out, a moment we find,
when we take a break and clear our mind. It's a chance to
reflect and calm our pace, learning from
our actions in this special space. When we make
mistakes, big or small, a time-out helps us
understand and recall the importance of kindness
and making things right, growing and
improving, shining our inner light.

U is for Umbrella, for rain or shine,
And Cma has so many, to keep her just fine.
When clouds gather and rain starts to fall,
C'ma has umbrellas prepared for the rainfall.

V is for Vote, a privilege we'll know when we turn eighteen, and our voices can grow. C'ma and PaPa explained its importance to me, that voting empowers us, and sets us free. When the time comes, we'll have a say in shaping our future in our own unique way.

W is for Why, our curious minds yearn,
to explore and discover, as we eagerly learn.
With wonder in our eyes, we question and ask,
"Why is the sky blue?"
"Why does time move fast?"
From morning till night, we're filled with intrigue,
seeking answers to puzzles, big and small, indeed.

23

X is for X-rays which are really neat.
Those are special pictures
that doctors can't beat. With
their strong power to see right through,
X-rays help diagnose and treat me and you.
E.B.B KIDS
E.B.B KIDS

When the day is winding down, and bedtime is near,
Y is for yawning when sleep time is here.
Yawning is spreading from one to another,
a gentle reminder to rest and recover.

Z is for zebras, with black and white stripes,
moving together, side by side. Their stripes provide
camouflage, blending with the herd,
a defense against predators, as nature preferred.

In Cma and Papa's house, we had so much fun,
Exploring each room from morning until sun.
They read us Cma's books, so lively and bright,
For brave little kids, she writes with all her might.

From A to Z, we learned and we played,
With Cma and Papa, lots of memories were made.
They taught us to be brave, to dream and to explore,
With love and support, we couldn't ask for more.

Thank you, Cma and Papa, for all that you do,
For sharing your wisdom and making us feel true.
We'll carry these lessons throughout our whole lives,
With courage and kindness, we will grow and thrive.
E.B.B
E.B.B
KIDS
E.B.B
KIDS

As we say goodbye to Cma and Papa's place,
We'll cherish the moments
and keep them in our grace.

We'll cherish those moments, forever and a day,
in our hearts, the memories will forever stay.
With love and imagination, we'll shine so bright,
carrying their lessons like stars in the night

E.B.B
KIDS
E.B.B
KIDS

The End
E.B.B
Kids
E.B.B
Kids

About the Author

Dr. Celestine McNeal is an incredible author, filled with love and passion. She has written a truly remarkable book, inspired by the joy and wonder she experiences through her beloved grandchildren. With a deep connection to the little ones in her life, she weaves captivating tales that ignite the imagination of both children and adults alike. In her book, Dr. McNeal creates enchanting narratives that transport readers to magical worlds, where valuable lessons are learned along the way. Her stories capture the innocence, curiosity, and boundless energy of childhood,resonating with readers of all ages. Dr. McNeal understands the importance of nurturing a child's imagination and fostering a love for reading.Through her writing,she aims to inspire young minds, encouraging them to dream big and explore their own creativity. She believes that books have the power to shape lives and open doors to endless possibilities.With her book, inspired by the enchanting spirit of her grandchildren,Dr. Celestine McNeal shares a piece of her heart with the world. She invites readers to embarkon a delightful journey, where love, laughter, and the joy of discovery await at every turn of the page.

www.ingramcontent.com/pod-product-compliance
Lightning Source LLC
Chambersburg PA
CBHW081057140726
48009CB00014B/228